50 Beyond Breadstick Recipes

By: Kelly Johnson

Table of Contents

- Garlic Parmesan Knots
- Cheddar Bay Biscuits
- Soft Pretzels
- Biscuit Bites
- Stuffed Cheese Breadsticks
- Parmesan Crusted Bread
- Focaccia with Rosemary
- Cinnamon Sugar Twists
- Herb-Crusted Pull-Apart Bread
- Pizza Dough Bites
- Jalapeño Cheddar Breadsticks
- Pita Bread with Hummus
- Cheesy Garlic Rolls
- Spinach and Cheese Swirls
- Olive Bread
- Potato Rolls
- Parmesan and Poppy Seed Bread
- Asiago Cheese Bread
- Chive and Cheddar Biscuits
- Roasted Garlic Focaccia
- Onion Rings with Spicy Sauce
- Sweet Potato Biscuits
- Zucchini Fritters
- Grilled Flatbreads
- Sourdough Pretzel Bites
- Pull-Apart Garlic Rolls
- Bread Machine Cinnamon Rolls
- Sun-Dried Tomato and Basil Bread
- Stuffed Spinach Rolls
- Roasted Vegetable Flatbread
- Garlic Cheese Bombs
- Bacon Cheddar Biscuits
- Cornbread Muffins
- Rye Bread
- Poppy Seed Breadsticks

- Sweet Cornbread with Honey Butter
- Asiago-Stuffed Bread
- Parmesan-Crusted Garlic Bread
- Crusty French Bread
- Baked Bagels
- Sweet Potato and Sage Biscuits
- Roasted Garlic and Herb Bread
- Mushroom-Stuffed Bread
- Grilled Naan Bread
- Stuffed Bread with Chicken and Spinach
- Pimento Cheese Biscuits
- Bacon-Wrapped Breadsticks
- Chia and Flaxseed Rolls
- Onion and Cheese Bread
- Tomato Basil Focaccia

Garlic Parmesan Knots

Ingredients:

- 1 package pizza dough (or homemade dough)
- 3 tablespoons butter, melted
- 3 garlic cloves, minced
- 1/4 cup grated Parmesan cheese
- 2 tablespoons fresh parsley, chopped
- Salt to taste

Instructions:

1. Preheat the oven to 375°F (190°C). Roll out the pizza dough into a rectangle and cut into strips.
2. Tie each strip into a knot and place on a baking sheet.
3. In a small bowl, combine melted butter, garlic, Parmesan, parsley, and salt. Brush the mixture over the dough knots.
4. Bake for 10-12 minutes until golden brown. Serve warm.

Cheddar Bay Biscuits

Ingredients:

- 2 cups all-purpose flour
- 1 tablespoon baking powder
- 1/2 teaspoon garlic powder
- 1/4 teaspoon salt
- 1/4 teaspoon black pepper
- 1/2 cup cold butter, cubed
- 1 cup shredded cheddar cheese
- 3/4 cup milk
- 2 tablespoons melted butter (for brushing)
- 1 tablespoon dried parsley (optional)

Instructions:

1. Preheat the oven to 425°F (220°C). In a large bowl, mix flour, baking powder, garlic powder, salt, and pepper.
2. Cut in the cold butter until the mixture resembles coarse crumbs. Stir in cheddar cheese.
3. Add milk and mix until just combined.
4. Drop spoonfuls of dough onto a greased baking sheet.
5. Bake for 12-15 minutes until golden brown. Brush with melted butter and sprinkle with parsley, if desired.

Soft Pretzels

Ingredients:

- 1 package active dry yeast
- 1 1/2 cups warm water
- 1 tablespoon sugar
- 4 cups all-purpose flour
- 1 teaspoon salt
- 2 tablespoons butter, melted
- 1/4 cup baking soda
- Coarse salt for sprinkling

Instructions:

1. In a bowl, dissolve yeast and sugar in warm water. Let sit for 5-10 minutes until bubbly.
2. Add flour, salt, and melted butter, and knead until smooth.
3. Let the dough rise for 1 hour, or until doubled in size.
4. Preheat the oven to 425°F (220°C). Boil a pot of water and add baking soda.
5. Divide the dough into portions, roll each into a rope, and form into pretzel shapes. Boil each pretzel for 30 seconds, then transfer to a baking sheet.
6. Sprinkle with coarse salt and bake for 12-15 minutes until golden brown.

Biscuit Bites

Ingredients:

- 2 cups all-purpose flour
- 1 tablespoon baking powder
- 1/2 teaspoon salt
- 1/2 teaspoon garlic powder
- 1/2 cup cold butter, cubed
- 3/4 cup milk
- 1/4 cup shredded cheese (optional)

Instructions:

1. Preheat the oven to 375°F (190°C). In a large bowl, mix flour, baking powder, salt, and garlic powder.
2. Cut in the cold butter until the mixture resembles coarse crumbs. Stir in milk and cheese, if using.
3. Drop spoonfuls of dough onto a greased baking sheet.
4. Bake for 10-12 minutes until golden brown.

Stuffed Cheese Breadsticks

Ingredients:

- 1 package pizza dough (or homemade dough)
- 1 cup shredded mozzarella cheese
- 1/4 cup grated Parmesan cheese
- 1 tablespoon garlic butter
- Marinara sauce for dipping

Instructions:

1. Preheat the oven to 375°F (190°C). Roll out pizza dough into a rectangle.
2. Sprinkle shredded mozzarella and Parmesan over half of the dough.
3. Fold the dough over the cheese and seal the edges. Cut into strips.
4. Twist each strip and place on a baking sheet. Brush with garlic butter.
5. Bake for 10-12 minutes until golden. Serve with marinara sauce for dipping.

Parmesan Crusted Bread

Ingredients:

- 1 loaf French bread
- 1/2 cup grated Parmesan cheese
- 1/4 cup butter, melted
- 2 garlic cloves, minced
- 1 tablespoon fresh parsley, chopped
- Salt to taste

Instructions:

1. Preheat the oven to 375°F (190°C). Slice the loaf of bread in half lengthwise.
2. In a small bowl, mix melted butter, garlic, Parmesan, parsley, and salt.
3. Spread the mixture over the cut sides of the bread.
4. Place on a baking sheet and bake for 10-12 minutes until golden and crispy.

Focaccia with Rosemary

Ingredients:

- 2 cups all-purpose flour
- 1 tablespoon active dry yeast
- 1/2 cup warm water
- 1 tablespoon olive oil
- 1 teaspoon salt
- 1 tablespoon fresh rosemary, chopped
- Coarse salt for sprinkling

Instructions:

1. Preheat the oven to 375°F (190°C). In a bowl, dissolve yeast in warm water and let sit for 5 minutes.
2. Add flour, olive oil, and salt. Knead until smooth and elastic.
3. Let the dough rise for 1 hour, or until doubled in size.
4. Roll out the dough onto a greased baking sheet, dimple the surface with your fingers, and sprinkle with rosemary and coarse salt.
5. Bake for 20-25 minutes until golden brown.

Cinnamon Sugar Twists

Ingredients:

- 1 package pizza dough (or homemade dough)
- 1/4 cup sugar
- 1 tablespoon cinnamon
- 1/4 cup butter, melted

Instructions:

1. Preheat the oven to 375°F (190°C). Roll out pizza dough into a rectangle.
2. In a small bowl, mix sugar and cinnamon.
3. Brush the dough with melted butter and sprinkle with cinnamon sugar.
4. Cut the dough into strips and twist each one.
5. Place on a baking sheet and bake for 10-12 minutes until golden and crispy.

Herb-Crusted Pull-Apart Bread

Ingredients:

- 1 loaf French bread
- 1/4 cup olive oil
- 2 teaspoons Italian seasoning
- 1/4 teaspoon garlic powder
- 1/4 cup grated Parmesan cheese
- Fresh parsley for garnish

Instructions:

1. Preheat the oven to 375°F (190°C). Slice the loaf of bread into cubes without cutting all the way through.
2. In a small bowl, mix olive oil, Italian seasoning, garlic powder, and Parmesan cheese.
3. Drizzle the mixture over the bread, ensuring it gets into the cracks.
4. Wrap the bread in foil and bake for 15-20 minutes. Garnish with fresh parsley.

Pizza Dough Bites

Ingredients:

- 1 package pizza dough (or homemade dough)
- 1/4 cup olive oil
- 1 tablespoon Italian seasoning
- 1/4 cup grated Parmesan cheese
- Marinara sauce for dipping

Instructions:

1. Preheat the oven to 375°F (190°C). Roll out pizza dough and cut into small squares.
2. Place the dough squares on a baking sheet and brush with olive oil.
3. Sprinkle with Italian seasoning and Parmesan cheese.
4. Bake for 8-10 minutes until golden brown. Serve with marinara sauce for dipping.

Jalapeño Cheddar Breadsticks

Ingredients:

- 1 package pizza dough (or homemade dough)
- 1 cup shredded cheddar cheese
- 2 jalapeños, seeded and finely chopped
- 2 tablespoons olive oil
- 1 tablespoon garlic powder
- Salt to taste

Instructions:

1. Preheat the oven to 375°F (190°C). Roll out pizza dough into a rectangle.
2. Sprinkle shredded cheddar cheese and chopped jalapeños over the dough.
3. Cut the dough into strips and twist each strip.
4. Place on a baking sheet and brush with olive oil. Sprinkle with garlic powder and salt.
5. Bake for 12-15 minutes until golden and crispy.

Pita Bread with Hummus

Ingredients for Pita Bread:

- 2 cups all-purpose flour
- 1 tablespoon olive oil
- 1 teaspoon active dry yeast
- 1/2 teaspoon salt
- 3/4 cup warm water

Instructions:

1. Preheat the oven to 475°F (245°C) and place a baking sheet or pizza stone in the oven.
2. In a bowl, combine flour, yeast, salt, and olive oil. Add warm water and knead until smooth.
3. Let the dough rise for 1 hour, then divide into small balls and roll each into a thin round.
4. Place the rounds on a hot baking sheet or pizza stone and bake for 3-5 minutes until puffed and golden.
5. Serve with your favorite hummus.

Cheesy Garlic Rolls

Ingredients:

- 1 package pizza dough (or homemade dough)
- 2 tablespoons butter, melted
- 3 garlic cloves, minced
- 1 cup shredded mozzarella cheese
- 1/4 cup grated Parmesan cheese
- 1 tablespoon fresh parsley, chopped

Instructions:

1. Preheat the oven to 375°F (190°C). Roll out the pizza dough and brush with melted butter.
2. Sprinkle minced garlic, mozzarella, Parmesan, and parsley over the dough.
3. Roll the dough into a log and slice it into rolls.
4. Arrange the rolls on a baking sheet and bake for 12-15 minutes until golden brown.

Spinach and Cheese Swirls

Ingredients:

- 1 package pizza dough (or homemade dough)
- 1 cup cooked spinach, squeezed dry and chopped
- 1/2 cup ricotta cheese
- 1/2 cup mozzarella cheese, shredded
- 1 tablespoon olive oil
- 1 tablespoon garlic powder

Instructions:

1. Preheat the oven to 375°F (190°C). Roll out the pizza dough into a rectangle.
2. Mix spinach, ricotta, mozzarella, and garlic powder in a bowl.
3. Spread the mixture evenly on the dough, then roll it up tightly.
4. Slice into rolls and place them on a baking sheet.
5. Bake for 15-20 minutes until golden. Serve warm.

Olive Bread

Ingredients:

- 2 1/2 cups all-purpose flour
- 1 packet active dry yeast
- 1/2 cup black olives, chopped
- 1/2 cup green olives, chopped
- 1 tablespoon olive oil
- 1 teaspoon salt
- 1 cup warm water

Instructions:

1. Preheat the oven to 375°F (190°C). In a bowl, combine flour, yeast, salt, and olive oil.
2. Add warm water and mix to form a dough. Knead until smooth, then let rise for 1 hour.
3. Gently fold in chopped olives and shape the dough into a loaf.
4. Place the loaf on a baking sheet and bake for 25-30 minutes until golden.

Potato Rolls

Ingredients:

- 2 cups mashed potatoes
- 3 cups all-purpose flour
- 1 tablespoon active dry yeast
- 1/4 cup sugar
- 1/4 cup butter, melted
- 1 teaspoon salt
- 3/4 cup warm water

Instructions:

1. Preheat the oven to 375°F (190°C). In a bowl, combine mashed potatoes, flour, yeast, sugar, salt, and melted butter.
2. Add warm water and mix to form a dough. Knead until smooth.
3. Let the dough rise for 1 hour, then divide into rolls and place on a greased baking sheet.
4. Bake for 12-15 minutes until golden brown. Serve warm.

Parmesan and Poppy Seed Bread

Ingredients:

- 2 1/2 cups all-purpose flour
- 1 tablespoon active dry yeast
- 1/4 cup Parmesan cheese, grated
- 1 tablespoon poppy seeds
- 1 tablespoon olive oil
- 1 teaspoon salt
- 1 cup warm water

Instructions:

1. Preheat the oven to 375°F (190°C). In a bowl, combine flour, yeast, salt, Parmesan, and poppy seeds.
2. Add warm water and olive oil, and knead until smooth.
3. Let the dough rise for 1 hour, then shape it into a loaf.
4. Place the dough on a baking sheet and bake for 25-30 minutes until golden.

Asiago Cheese Bread

Ingredients:

- 3 cups all-purpose flour
- 1 tablespoon active dry yeast
- 1/2 cup Asiago cheese, shredded
- 1 teaspoon garlic powder
- 1 tablespoon olive oil
- 1 cup warm water
- 1 teaspoon salt

Instructions:

1. Preheat the oven to 375°F (190°C). In a bowl, combine flour, yeast, garlic powder, salt, and Asiago cheese.
2. Add warm water and olive oil, then knead until smooth.
3. Let the dough rise for 1 hour. Shape the dough into a loaf.
4. Place on a greased baking sheet and bake for 25-30 minutes, or until golden brown.

Chive and Cheddar Biscuits

Ingredients:

- 2 cups all-purpose flour
- 1 tablespoon baking powder
- 1/2 teaspoon salt
- 1/2 cup cold butter, cubed
- 1 cup sharp cheddar cheese, shredded
- 2 tablespoons fresh chives, chopped
- 3/4 cup milk

Instructions:

1. Preheat the oven to 425°F (220°C). In a bowl, combine flour, baking powder, and salt.
2. Cut in the cold butter until the mixture resembles coarse crumbs.
3. Stir in cheddar cheese, chives, and milk to form a dough.
4. Drop spoonfuls of dough onto a greased baking sheet.
5. Bake for 10-12 minutes until golden.

Roasted Garlic Focaccia

Ingredients:

- 2 cups all-purpose flour
- 1 tablespoon active dry yeast
- 1/2 cup warm water
- 2 tablespoons olive oil
- 1 bulb garlic, roasted and mashed
- 1 tablespoon fresh rosemary, chopped
- Salt to taste

Instructions:

1. Preheat the oven to 375°F (190°C). In a bowl, dissolve yeast in warm water and let sit for 5 minutes.
2. Add flour and olive oil, and knead until smooth. Let rise for 1 hour.
3. Preheat a pan with olive oil and spread the dough on it. Top with roasted garlic, rosemary, and salt.
4. Bake for 20-25 minutes until golden and crispy.

Onion Rings with Spicy Sauce

Ingredients for Onion Rings:

- 2 large onions, sliced into rings
- 1 cup flour
- 1 teaspoon paprika
- 1/2 teaspoon garlic powder
- 1/2 teaspoon salt
- 1/2 teaspoon pepper
- 1 cup buttermilk
- 1 cup breadcrumbs
- Vegetable oil for frying

For Spicy Sauce:

- 1/2 cup mayonnaise
- 2 tablespoons sriracha sauce
- 1 tablespoon ketchup
- 1/2 teaspoon garlic powder

Instructions:

1. In a bowl, combine flour, paprika, garlic powder, salt, and pepper.
2. Dip onion rings into buttermilk, then dredge in the flour mixture followed by breadcrumbs.
3. Heat oil in a deep pan to 375°F (190°C). Fry onion rings in batches until golden brown.
4. In a small bowl, mix mayonnaise, sriracha, ketchup, and garlic powder to make the spicy sauce.
5. Drain onion rings on paper towels and serve with the spicy sauce.

Sweet Potato Biscuits

Ingredients:

- 1 cup mashed sweet potato (cooked)
- 2 cups all-purpose flour
- 1 tablespoon baking powder
- 1/2 teaspoon salt
- 1/2 teaspoon cinnamon
- 1/2 cup cold butter, cubed
- 3/4 cup milk

Instructions:

1. Preheat the oven to 375°F (190°C). In a bowl, mix flour, baking powder, salt, and cinnamon.
2. Cut in the cold butter until the mixture resembles coarse crumbs.
3. Stir in mashed sweet potato and milk until just combined.
4. Drop spoonfuls of dough onto a greased baking sheet.
5. Bake for 15-18 minutes until golden brown.

Zucchini Fritters

Ingredients:

- 2 medium zucchinis, grated
- 1/2 cup all-purpose flour
- 2 eggs
- 1/4 cup Parmesan cheese
- 1/4 teaspoon garlic powder
- Salt and pepper to taste
- Olive oil for frying

Instructions:

1. Place grated zucchini in a clean kitchen towel and squeeze out excess moisture.
2. In a bowl, mix zucchini, flour, eggs, Parmesan, garlic powder, salt, and pepper.
3. Heat olive oil in a pan over medium heat. Scoop spoonfuls of the mixture into the pan and flatten slightly.
4. Cook for 3-4 minutes per side until golden brown. Serve with a dipping sauce or yogurt.

Grilled Flatbreads

Ingredients:

- 2 cups all-purpose flour
- 1 tablespoon olive oil
- 1 teaspoon active dry yeast
- 3/4 cup warm water
- 1 teaspoon salt
- 1 tablespoon honey

Instructions:

1. In a bowl, dissolve yeast and honey in warm water. Let sit for 5 minutes to activate.
2. Add flour, salt, and olive oil. Stir to form a dough, then knead for about 8 minutes.
3. Let the dough rise for 1 hour. Preheat the grill to medium-high heat.
4. Roll the dough into small rounds and grill for 2-3 minutes on each side until lightly charred.
5. Serve warm with toppings or dips.

Sourdough Pretzel Bites

Ingredients:

- 1 1/2 cups sourdough starter
- 2 cups all-purpose flour
- 1 tablespoon sugar
- 1 teaspoon salt
- 1 tablespoon baking soda
- 1/4 cup water
- Coarse salt for sprinkling

Instructions:

1. Preheat the oven to 375°F (190°C). In a bowl, mix sourdough starter, flour, sugar, and salt to form a dough.
2. Divide the dough into small pieces and roll into bites.
3. In a pot, boil water with baking soda. Drop the pretzel bites into the boiling water for 30 seconds, then transfer to a baking sheet.
4. Sprinkle with coarse salt and bake for 15-18 minutes until golden.

Pull-Apart Garlic Rolls

Ingredients:

- 1 package pizza dough (or homemade dough)
- 4 tablespoons butter, melted
- 3 garlic cloves, minced
- 1 tablespoon fresh parsley, chopped
- Salt to taste

Instructions:

1. Preheat the oven to 375°F (190°C). Roll out the pizza dough and cut it into small squares.
2. Arrange the squares in a baking dish.
3. In a small bowl, combine melted butter, garlic, parsley, and salt. Brush the mixture over the dough.
4. Bake for 15-18 minutes until golden and fluffy.

Bread Machine Cinnamon Rolls

Ingredients:

- 1 cup warm milk
- 1/4 cup sugar
- 1 packet active dry yeast
- 3 cups all-purpose flour
- 1/2 teaspoon salt
- 1/4 cup butter, softened
- 1 egg
- 1 tablespoon cinnamon
- 1/2 cup brown sugar

Instructions:

1. In the bread machine, combine warm milk, sugar, and yeast. Let sit for 5 minutes to activate the yeast.
2. Add flour, salt, butter, and egg to the bread machine. Set to the dough cycle.
3. Roll out the dough, spread with butter, and sprinkle with cinnamon and brown sugar.
4. Roll up the dough and cut into rolls. Let rise for 30 minutes.
5. Bake at 375°F (190°C) for 15-18 minutes.

Sun-Dried Tomato and Basil Bread

Ingredients:

- 2 1/2 cups all-purpose flour
- 1 tablespoon active dry yeast
- 1/2 cup sun-dried tomatoes, chopped
- 1/4 cup fresh basil, chopped
- 1 teaspoon salt
- 1 cup warm water
- 2 tablespoons olive oil

Instructions:

1. In a bowl, dissolve yeast in warm water and let sit for 5 minutes.
2. Add flour, salt, olive oil, sun-dried tomatoes, and basil. Knead until smooth and let rise for 1 hour.
3. Shape the dough into a loaf and place it in a greased loaf pan. Let rise for another 30 minutes.
4. Bake at 375°F (190°C) for 25-30 minutes until golden.

Stuffed Spinach Rolls

Ingredients:

- 1 package pizza dough (or homemade dough)
- 2 cups spinach, cooked and chopped
- 1/2 cup ricotta cheese
- 1/2 cup mozzarella cheese
- 1 tablespoon garlic powder
- Salt and pepper to taste

Instructions:

1. Preheat the oven to 375°F (190°C). Roll out the pizza dough into a rectangle.
2. Mix spinach, ricotta, mozzarella, garlic powder, salt, and pepper in a bowl.
3. Spread the mixture over the dough and roll it up tightly.
4. Slice the roll into small sections and place them on a baking sheet.
5. Bake for 15-20 minutes until golden brown.

Roasted Vegetable Flatbread

Ingredients:

- 1 package pizza dough (or homemade dough)
- 1 zucchini, sliced
- 1 bell pepper, sliced
- 1 red onion, sliced
- 2 tablespoons olive oil
- Salt and pepper to taste
- 1/4 cup feta cheese, crumbled

Instructions:

1. Preheat the oven to 400°F (200°C). Roll out the pizza dough and place on a baking sheet.
2. Toss zucchini, bell pepper, and onion with olive oil, salt, and pepper.
3. Arrange the vegetables on the dough and sprinkle with feta cheese.
4. Bake for 15-18 minutes until the dough is golden and the vegetables are tender.

Garlic Cheese Bombs

Ingredients:

- 1 package pizza dough (or homemade dough)
- 1 cup shredded mozzarella cheese
- 4 tablespoons butter, melted
- 2 garlic cloves, minced
- 1 tablespoon parsley, chopped

Instructions:

1. Preheat the oven to 375°F (190°C). Roll out the pizza dough and cut into small squares.
2. Place a cube of cheese in the center of each square, then roll it into a ball.
3. Arrange the balls on a greased baking sheet. In a small bowl, mix melted butter, garlic, and parsley, and brush over the dough balls.
4. Bake for 12-15 minutes until golden and gooey inside.

Bacon Cheddar Biscuits

Ingredients:

- 2 cups all-purpose flour
- 1 tablespoon baking powder
- 1/2 teaspoon salt
- 1/4 cup cold butter, cubed
- 1 cup shredded cheddar cheese
- 1/2 cup cooked bacon, crumbled
- 3/4 cup milk

Instructions:

1. Preheat the oven to 400°F (200°C). In a bowl, mix flour, baking powder, and salt.
2. Cut in cold butter until the mixture resembles coarse crumbs. Stir in cheddar cheese and bacon.
3. Add milk and stir until just combined.
4. Drop spoonfuls of dough onto a greased baking sheet and bake for 12-15 minutes until golden brown.

Cornbread Muffins

Ingredients:

- 1 cup cornmeal
- 1 cup all-purpose flour
- 1 tablespoon baking powder
- 1/2 teaspoon salt
- 1/4 cup sugar
- 1/2 cup milk
- 2 eggs
- 1/4 cup melted butter
- 1/4 cup honey (optional)

Instructions:

1. Preheat the oven to 375°F (190°C). Grease or line a muffin tin.
2. In a bowl, mix cornmeal, flour, baking powder, salt, and sugar.
3. In a separate bowl, whisk together milk, eggs, melted butter, and honey (if using).
4. Combine wet and dry ingredients and stir until just combined.
5. Spoon the batter into the muffin tin and bake for 18-20 minutes until golden and a toothpick comes out clean.

Rye Bread

Ingredients:

- 2 cups rye flour
- 1 1/2 cups all-purpose flour
- 1 tablespoon caraway seeds (optional)
- 2 teaspoons salt
- 1 tablespoon sugar
- 2 teaspoons active dry yeast
- 1 1/2 cups warm water
- 2 tablespoons olive oil

Instructions:

1. In a bowl, combine rye flour, all-purpose flour, caraway seeds, salt, and sugar.
2. Dissolve yeast in warm water and let sit for 5 minutes until bubbly.
3. Add yeast mixture and olive oil to the dry ingredients. Stir to form a dough.
4. Knead the dough for 8-10 minutes, then let rise for 1 hour.
5. Shape the dough into a loaf and place it in a greased loaf pan. Let rise for another 30 minutes.
6. Preheat the oven to 375°F (190°C) and bake for 30-35 minutes until the bread sounds hollow when tapped.

Poppy Seed Breadsticks

Ingredients:

- 1 package pizza dough (or homemade dough)
- 2 tablespoons olive oil
- 1 tablespoon poppy seeds
- 1 tablespoon garlic powder
- Salt to taste

Instructions:

1. Preheat the oven to 375°F (190°C). Roll out the pizza dough into a rectangle and cut it into strips.
2. Brush each strip with olive oil, then sprinkle with poppy seeds, garlic powder, and salt.
3. Twist the dough strips and place them on a baking sheet.
4. Bake for 12-15 minutes until golden and crispy.

Sweet Cornbread with Honey Butter

Ingredients for Cornbread:

- 1 cup cornmeal
- 1 cup all-purpose flour
- 1 tablespoon baking powder
- 1/2 teaspoon salt
- 1/2 cup sugar
- 1 cup milk
- 2 eggs
- 1/4 cup melted butter

For Honey Butter:

- 1/4 cup butter, softened
- 2 tablespoons honey

Instructions:

1. Preheat the oven to 375°F (190°C). Grease a baking dish.
2. In a bowl, mix cornmeal, flour, baking powder, salt, and sugar.
3. In another bowl, whisk together milk, eggs, and melted butter. Combine with the dry ingredients and mix until smooth.
4. Pour the batter into the baking dish and bake for 25-30 minutes until golden.
5. For honey butter, mix softened butter and honey until smooth. Serve with cornbread.

Asiago-Stuffed Bread

Ingredients:

- 1 package pizza dough (or homemade dough)
- 1 1/2 cups shredded Asiago cheese
- 1 tablespoon olive oil
- 1 teaspoon garlic powder
- Salt and pepper to taste

Instructions:

1. Preheat the oven to 375°F (190°C). Roll out the pizza dough into a rectangle.
2. Sprinkle shredded Asiago cheese evenly over half of the dough.
3. Fold the dough over the cheese and seal the edges. Cut slits in the top of the dough.
4. Brush with olive oil, then sprinkle with garlic powder, salt, and pepper.
5. Bake for 20-25 minutes until golden brown.

Parmesan-Crusted Garlic Bread

Ingredients:

- 1 loaf French bread
- 1/4 cup butter, softened
- 2 garlic cloves, minced
- 1/2 cup grated Parmesan cheese
- 1 tablespoon fresh parsley, chopped
- Salt to taste

Instructions:

1. Preheat the oven to 375°F (190°C). Slice the loaf of bread in half lengthwise.
2. In a small bowl, mix softened butter, garlic, Parmesan cheese, parsley, and salt.
3. Spread the mixture evenly on the cut sides of the bread.
4. Place on a baking sheet and bake for 10-12 minutes until golden and crispy.

Crusty French Bread

Ingredients:

- 3 cups all-purpose flour
- 1 tablespoon active dry yeast
- 1 teaspoon salt
- 1 tablespoon sugar
- 1 cup warm water
- 2 tablespoons olive oil

Instructions:

1. Preheat the oven to 400°F (200°C). In a bowl, dissolve yeast and sugar in warm water. Let sit for 5 minutes.
2. Add flour, salt, and olive oil, and knead until smooth.
3. Let the dough rise for 1 hour. Punch down the dough and shape it into a loaf.
4. Place the loaf on a greased baking sheet and let rise for another 30 minutes.
5. Bake for 25-30 minutes until golden and crusty.

Baked Bagels

Ingredients:

- 3 cups all-purpose flour
- 1 tablespoon sugar
- 1 tablespoon active dry yeast
- 1 teaspoon salt
- 1 1/4 cups warm water
- 1 tablespoon vegetable oil
- 1 egg, beaten (for egg wash)
- Toppings: sesame seeds, poppy seeds, or salt (optional)

Instructions:

1. Preheat the oven to 375°F (190°C). In a bowl, dissolve yeast and sugar in warm water. Let sit for 5 minutes.
2. Add flour and salt to form a dough. Knead until smooth, then let rise for 1 hour.
3. Shape the dough into bagels and place them in simmering water for 2-3 minutes. Remove and let cool slightly.
4. Brush with beaten egg and sprinkle with your choice of toppings.
5. Bake for 20-25 minutes until golden brown.

Sweet Potato and Sage Biscuits

Ingredients:

- 1 cup mashed sweet potato
- 2 cups all-purpose flour
- 1 tablespoon baking powder
- 1/2 teaspoon salt
- 1/4 teaspoon cinnamon
- 1/4 cup cold butter, cubed
- 1 tablespoon fresh sage, chopped
- 3/4 cup milk

Instructions:

1. Preheat the oven to 375°F (190°C). In a bowl, combine flour, baking powder, salt, and cinnamon.
2. Cut in cold butter until the mixture resembles coarse crumbs.
3. Add mashed sweet potato, sage, and milk. Stir to form a dough.
4. Drop spoonfuls of dough onto a baking sheet and bake for 12-15 minutes until golden brown.

Roasted Garlic and Herb Bread

Ingredients:

- 2 1/2 cups all-purpose flour
- 1 tablespoon active dry yeast
- 1 teaspoon salt
- 1 tablespoon olive oil
- 1 cup warm water
- 1 bulb garlic, roasted and mashed
- 1 tablespoon fresh thyme, chopped

Instructions:

1. Preheat the oven to 375°F (190°C). In a bowl, dissolve yeast in warm water and let sit for 5 minutes.
2. Add flour, salt, olive oil, roasted garlic, and thyme. Knead until smooth and let rise for 1 hour.
3. Shape dough into a loaf and let rise for 30 minutes.
4. Bake for 25-30 minutes until golden.

Mushroom-Stuffed Bread

Ingredients:

- 1 package pizza dough (or homemade dough)
- 1 cup mushrooms, chopped
- 1/4 cup onion, chopped
- 2 tablespoons olive oil
- 1/2 cup ricotta cheese
- 1/2 cup shredded mozzarella cheese
- Salt and pepper to taste

Instructions:

1. Preheat the oven to 375°F (190°C). In a pan, heat olive oil and sauté onions and mushrooms until soft. Let cool.
2. Roll out the pizza dough and spread ricotta cheese in the center.
3. Top with the mushroom mixture and mozzarella cheese. Roll up the dough and seal the edges.
4. Bake for 25-30 minutes until golden brown. Serve warm.

Grilled Naan Bread

Ingredients:

- 2 cups all-purpose flour
- 1 tablespoon sugar
- 1 teaspoon active dry yeast
- 1/2 teaspoon salt
- 1/4 cup plain yogurt
- 1/4 cup warm water
- 2 tablespoons olive oil
- 2 tablespoons melted butter (for brushing)

Instructions:

1. In a bowl, combine warm water, yeast, and sugar. Let sit for 5 minutes to activate.
2. Add flour, salt, yogurt, and olive oil to the yeast mixture and stir to form a dough.
3. Knead the dough for 8-10 minutes until smooth. Let it rise for 1 hour.
4. Preheat a grill to medium-high heat. Divide the dough into small portions and roll each into a thin circle.
5. Grill each naan for 1-2 minutes per side until lightly charred. Brush with melted butter and serve warm.

Stuffed Bread with Chicken and Spinach

Ingredients:

- 1 package pizza dough (or homemade dough)
- 2 chicken breasts, cooked and shredded
- 1 cup cooked spinach, chopped
- 1/2 cup ricotta cheese
- 1/4 cup mozzarella cheese, shredded
- 1 tablespoon olive oil
- 1 teaspoon garlic powder
- Salt and pepper to taste

Instructions:

1. Preheat the oven to 375°F (190°C). Roll out the pizza dough into a rectangle.
2. In a bowl, combine shredded chicken, spinach, ricotta, mozzarella, garlic powder, salt, and pepper.
3. Spread the mixture over half of the dough, then fold the dough over and seal the edges.
4. Brush with olive oil and bake for 20-25 minutes until golden and crispy.

Pimento Cheese Biscuits

Ingredients:

- 2 cups all-purpose flour
- 1 tablespoon baking powder
- 1/2 teaspoon salt
- 1/4 teaspoon cayenne pepper
- 1/2 cup cold butter, cubed
- 1 cup shredded sharp cheddar cheese
- 1/2 cup pimento cheese spread
- 3/4 cup milk

Instructions:

1. Preheat the oven to 400°F (200°C). In a bowl, mix flour, baking powder, salt, and cayenne pepper.
2. Cut in cold butter until the mixture resembles coarse crumbs.
3. Stir in cheddar cheese and pimento cheese spread. Add milk and mix until just combined.
4. Drop spoonfuls of dough onto a greased baking sheet.
5. Bake for 10-12 minutes until golden and fluffy.

Bacon-Wrapped Breadsticks

Ingredients:

- 1 package pizza dough (or homemade dough)
- 8 slices bacon
- 1 tablespoon olive oil
- 1 teaspoon garlic powder
- 1/4 cup grated Parmesan cheese

Instructions:

1. Preheat the oven to 400°F (200°C). Roll out the pizza dough and cut into long strips.
2. Wrap each dough strip with a slice of bacon.
3. Place the bacon-wrapped dough strips on a baking sheet. Brush with olive oil and sprinkle with garlic powder and Parmesan cheese.
4. Bake for 12-15 minutes until golden brown and the bacon is crispy.

Chia and Flaxseed Rolls

Ingredients:

- 2 cups all-purpose flour
- 1 tablespoon active dry yeast
- 1/4 cup chia seeds
- 2 tablespoons flaxseeds
- 1 teaspoon salt
- 1 tablespoon olive oil
- 1 cup warm water
- 1 tablespoon honey

Instructions:

1. In a bowl, dissolve yeast and honey in warm water. Let sit for 5 minutes.
2. Add flour, chia seeds, flaxseeds, salt, and olive oil. Stir to form a dough.
3. Knead the dough for 8-10 minutes, then let rise for 1 hour.
4. Divide the dough into small portions, shape into rolls, and place on a baking sheet.
5. Bake at 375°F (190°C) for 15-20 minutes until golden brown.

Onion and Cheese Bread

Ingredients:

- 2 cups all-purpose flour
- 1 tablespoon baking powder
- 1/2 teaspoon salt
- 1/4 cup grated Parmesan cheese
- 1/2 cup shredded cheddar cheese
- 1 onion, chopped
- 1/4 cup olive oil
- 1 cup milk

Instructions:

1. Preheat the oven to 375°F (190°C). In a bowl, mix flour, baking powder, salt, Parmesan, and cheddar cheese.
2. Add chopped onion, olive oil, and milk. Stir until combined.
3. Pour the batter into a greased loaf pan and bake for 25-30 minutes until golden and cooked through.
4. Let cool slightly before slicing and serving.

Tomato Basil Focaccia

Ingredients:

- 2 1/2 cups all-purpose flour
- 1 tablespoon active dry yeast
- 1 teaspoon salt
- 1 tablespoon olive oil
- 1 cup warm water
- 1/2 cup cherry tomatoes, halved
- 1/4 cup fresh basil, chopped
- 1 tablespoon olive oil (for drizzling)
- Coarse salt for sprinkling

Instructions:

1. Preheat the oven to 375°F (190°C). In a bowl, dissolve yeast in warm water. Let sit for 5 minutes.
2. Add flour, salt, and olive oil. Knead until smooth, then let rise for 1 hour.
3. Roll the dough out on a greased baking sheet. Press halved tomatoes into the dough and sprinkle with basil.
4. Drizzle with olive oil, sprinkle with coarse salt, and bake for 20-25 minutes until golden.

www.ingramcontent.com/pod-product-compliance
Lightning Source LLC
LaVergne TN
LVHW081331060526
838201LV00055B/2582